GRADES 1-3

STORYWRITING

LINDA BETH POLON

Good Year Books

An Imprint of Pearson Learning

Good Year Books

are available for most basic curriculum subjects plus many enrichment areas. For more Good Year Books, contact your local bookseller or educational dealer. For a complete catalog with information about other Good Year Books, please write to:

Good Year Books
299 Jefferson Road
Parsippany, NJ 07054

Design and Illustration: Street Level Studio
Editor: Laura Layton Strom
Editorial Manager: Suzanne Beason
Executive Editor: Judith Adams
Publisher: Rosemary Calicchio

ISBN 0-673-57580-2

1 2 3 4 5 6 7 8 9 – ML – 06 05 04 03 02 01 00 99

TABLE OF CONTENTS

HOW TO USE THIS BOOK

Storywriting, Grades 1–3, is designed to make writing fun for young children. For many this will be their first chance to express themselves through writing. As they write simple sentences and brief stories, they should feel absolutely unrestricted and free to soar with their imaginations. Their confidence will grow as they learn and so will their joy in sharing their thoughts and ideas.

The writing activities are divided into themes, as shown in the Table of Contents. Feel free to present the themes in any order that supports your teaching goals.

Beginning writers should be expected to write a sentence or two, while more advanced writers should be encouraged to write as much as they can. It is always helpful for you, the teacher, to read each page aloud and answer any questions students might have before they start writing.

At the completion of a writing assignment or theme, students can share their writings in a whole group class activity or in a small group. These sharing sessions are most effective when held regularly.

As an extension activity, *Storywriting, Grades 1–3* includes a Teachable Moments Skill List. This list is comprised of writing and grammar skills that can be used at your discretion with any of the writing activities. The list can be used to teach or to reinforce previously learned skills. For example, if your class is studying plural nouns, perhaps you would emphasize skill #11 (plural nouns) when assigning the writing activity. For more on Teachable Moments, see the next page.

TEACHABLE MOMENTS

A special feature of this book is the Teachable Moments Skill List, p. 3. In this list are skills that can be taught with any of the writing activities, depending on what is being taught "at the moment." This is purely an extension activity and can be used at your discretion.

The Teachable Moments Skill List can be used to teach or to reinforce previously learned skills. It will be up to you, as the teacher, to choose the teachable moment skill and then assign it to your students.

First, assign a creative writing exercise. When the assignment is complete, select a skill from the Teachable Moments Skill List. Teach or review the skill, and then have children practice the skill by proofreading what they have written, checking for usage. If children have not used the skill in their story, have them rewrite a sentence or two at the bottom of the page to illustrate their understanding of the skill.

For example, suppose you have just taught plural nouns, skill #11. A child proofreads her story and finds only singular nouns. To do the extension activity, she should lift a sentence or two (your option) out of her story, rewriting it at the bottom of the page to incorporate two (you choose the number) plural nouns. The new sentences are not to be incorporated into the story. They are merely for practice.

> original story: Her dog followed her to school.
> revision: Two dogs followed her to school.
>
> original story: I lost my baseball.
> revision: I lost many baseballs.

This extension of the creative writing process will not only help teach the skills studied, but it will also give children valuable practice in reading and proofreading what they have written. Additionally, children will begin to understand the role of different parts of speech and the makeup of grammatically correct sentences. This solid foundation will serve them well in the future as they continue to study language and grammar in the later elementary grades.

TEACHABLE MOMENTS SKILL LIST

1. Each sentence begins with a capital letter.

2. Leave a little space between words within a sentence and a slightly larger space between sentences.

3. A telling sentence (statement) tells something and ends with a period.
   Examples: **The sand is warm. The hospital is busy.**

4. An asking sentence (question) asks something and ends with a question mark.
   Examples: **How are you today? Can I go to the park?**

5. An exclamation is a sentence that shows strong feeling or surprise and ends with an exclamation mark.
   Examples: **Summer vacation is here! My pet turtle died!**

6. A command is a sentence that tells an order and ends with a period.
   Examples: **Sit down. Write neatly.**

7. The subject of a sentence is usually found in the first part of the sentence and tells who or what the sentence is about.
   Examples: <u>**The cat**</u> **meowed at the dog.** <u>**The rain**</u> **did not stop all day.**

8. The predicate of a sentence comes after the subject and tells what the subject does.
   Examples: **The cat** <u>**meowed at the dog.**</u> **The rain** <u>**did not stop all day.**</u>

9. Nouns are words that name a person (*woman*), place (*school*), or thing (*ball*).

10. Singular nouns name one person *(girl)*, place *(garden)*, or thing (ball).

11. Plural nouns name more than one person (*boys*), place (*homes*), or thing *(doors)*.

12. For irregular plural nouns that end in the letters *s, ss, sh, ch,* or *x*, add the letters *es* to make more than one.
    Examples: **class—classes, box—boxes, beach—beaches**

For nouns that end with a consonant and the letter *y*, change the *y* to *i* and then add *es* to form the plural.

Examples: **family—families, cherry—cherries**

Some words do not follow these rules.

Examples: **mouse—mice, man—men, woman—women, foot—feet, tooth—teeth**

13. Proper nouns name a particular person, place or thing and must be capitalized.

    Examples: **girl—Courtney, city—Los Angeles, state—Illinois, country—United States, thing—Statue of Liberty**

    Also capitalized are courtesy or professional titles (*Mr. Wilson, Dr. Vincent Johnson*), days of the week (*Wednesday*), and months (*October*).

14. A verb is found in the predicate and tells what someone or something does.

    Example: **The car <u>speeds</u> down the street.**

    The present tense of a verb tells about an action that is happening now.
    Example: **Suzie <u>looks</u> at Stan.** For verbs where the present tense ends in the letters *ch, s, sh, ss*, or *x*, add *es*.
    Examples: **teach—teaches, dress—dresses.**

    The past tense of the verb tells about an action that already happened at a particular time.
    Examples: **I watched TV all day. I danced in the show.**

    Instead of adding the letters *ed* to form the past tense, some verbs are irregular.
    Examples: **come—came, do—did, eat—ate, go—went, run—ran, see—saw**

15. An adjective is a word that tells about a person, place, or thing.

    Examples: **The <u>blue</u> house is where I live. My <u>happy</u> friend gave me a smile. The <u>leaky</u> faucet needs to be fixed. The <u>tall</u> building was next to my school.**

16. An adverb tells about verbs and often ends in the letters *ly*.
    Examples: **I talk <u>rapidly</u>. Ben works <u>hard</u>.**

    An adverb can also tell when an action is done.
    Examples: **I lost my homework <u>yesterday</u>. <u>Tomorrow</u>, I'll clean my room.**

17. A contraction is a shortened form of two words. An apostrophe takes the place of the missing letters.
    Examples: **is not—isn't, has not—hasn't, were not—weren't**

    Some contractions are irregular.
    Examples: **I will—I'll, you will—you'll, he will—he'll, they will—they'll, we will—we'll, have not—haven't**

18. A compound word is a word that is made up of two words.
    Examples: **homework, notebook, chalkboard**

19. Synonyms are words that have similar meaning.
    Examples: **happy—glad, little—small**

20. Antonyms are words that mean the opposite.
    Examples: **tall—short, hot—cold**

21. A pronoun is a word that is found in the subject of a sentence and takes the place of a noun. Pronouns include the words *I, you, he, she, it, we*, and *they*.
    Examples: **Allison and Jason were best friends. *They* were best friends. Felipe likes oranges. *He* likes oranges.**

22. An object pronoun is used in the predicate part of a sentence. It takes the place of a noun. Object pronouns include the words *me, you, him, her, it, us*, and *them*.
    Examples: **Tom calls *him*. They gave it to *us*.**

FEELINGS

HOW ARE YOU FEELING?, PART I

Name _____   Date _____

Sometimes we feel happy. Other times we feel sad. We have many different types of feelings—even in one day! Draw a face in each box to show what the feeling listed looks like on your face. Then fill in the blanks at the right to tell what makes you feel this way.

1.   happy

I feel happy when _____

_____

_____

2.   bored

I feel bored when _____

_____

_____

3.   lonely

I feel lonely when _____

_____

_____

FEELINGS

HOW ARE YOU FEELING?, PART 2

Name _____   Date _____

Sometimes we feel happy. Other times we feel sad. We have
many different types of feelings—even in one day! Draw a
face in each box to show what the feeling listed looks
like on your face. Then fill in the blanks at the right to
tell what makes you feel this way.

1.   scared

I feel scared
when _____

_____

_____

2.   excited

I feel excited
when _____

_____

_____

3.   angry

I feel angry
when _____

_____

_____

HOW ARE YOU FEELING?, PART 3

Name _____   Date _____

Sometimes we feel happy. Other times we feel sad. We have many different types of feelings—even in one day! Draw a face in each box to show what the feeling listed looks like on your face. Then fill in the blanks at the right to tell what makes you feel this way.

1.   smart

I feel smart
when _____

_____

_____

2.   silly

I feel silly
when _____

_____

_____

3.   loved

I feel loved
when _____

_____

_____

HOW WOULD YOU FEEL IF..., PART I

Name _____ Date _____

1. How would you feel if you saw someone taking something that belonged to you?

    I would feel _____

    because _____

    _____

2. How would you feel if you fell off your chair in class?

    I would feel _____

    because _____

    _____

3. How would you feel if your teacher put a happy-face sticker or symbol on your work?

    I would feel _____

    because _____

    _____

FEELINGS

HOW WOULD YOU FEEL IF..., PART 2

Name _____ Date _____

1. How would you feel if you were the last one picked to be on a team?

    I would feel _____

    because _____

    _____

2. How would you feel if you answered a question correctly?

    I would feel _____

    because _____

    _____

3. How would you feel if you helped your team win a game?

    I would feel _____

    because _____

    _____

FEELINGS

TALK ABOUT IT

Name _____   Date _____

Tell what you would do in the following situations. Remember that when
something is not going well for you at school, it is best to talk about it.

1. Tell what you'd do if your pencil box was missing.

2. Tell what you'd do if a child bumped into you and you thought it was
   on purpose.

3. Tell what you'd do if you saw that your
   dessert was missing from your lunch
   box, and you thought you knew who
   took it.

WRITE ABOUT YOUR FAMILY

Name _____   Date _____

1. What do you like best about your family?

2. Describe a favorite family meal.

3. Draw a picture of your family. Write each person's name next to his or her picture.

FEELINGS

EXPRESSING FEELINGS

Name _____   Date _____

How would you solve the following problems?

1. A friend tells you that you have hurt his or her feelings.

2. A friend is having a bad day and is taking it out on you.

ANIMALS, ANIMALS

IF I RAN THE ZOO

Name _____   Date _____

Pretend you are the boss of a zoo. Name four animals you would want in your zoo and why.

1. _____   Why? _____
   name

   _____

   _____

2. _____   Why? _____
   name

   _____

   _____

3. _____   Why? _____
   name

   _____

   _____

4. _____   Why? _____
   name

   _____

   _____

ANIMALS, ANIMALS

CREATE YOUR OWN ANIMAL

Name _____   Date _____

Pretend you are a scientist and you are able to invent new animals. Invent
an animal. Create your new animal by combining two different animals, for
example, half giraffe and half zebra. Name your new animal, tell about it,
and then draw a picture of it on the next page.

My animal's name is _____

and it is part _____

and part _____.

My animal is special because _____

_____

_____

_____

_____

_____

_____

CREATE YOUR OWN ANIMAL

Name _____   Date _____

ANIMALS, ANIMALS

YOUR PET

Name _____   Date _____

Answer the questions below about one of your pets. If you don't have a pet, write about one you would like to have.

1. What is the name of your pet? _____

2. Draw a picture of your pet.

3. How do you take care of your pet? _____

_____

_____

4. How do you show your pet you love him or her? _____

_____

_____

ANIMALS, ANIMALS

WHAT'S YOUR FAVORITE ANIMAL?

Name _____   Date _____

1. What is your favorite animal and why?

2. Look in a book and read about your favorite animal. Write two or three interesting facts about your animal.

3. Draw a picture of your favorite animal.

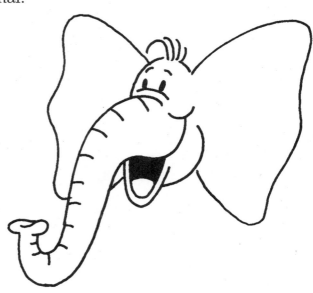

ANIMALS, ANIMALS

ANIMAL STORY

Name _____ Date _____

On the lines below, write a story about you and your pet. If you don't have
a pet, write about one you would like to have. You and your pet can go on
an adventure, take a trip, solve a mystery, or do something else. Have fun
writing your story! Then draw a picture of you and your pet in the box.

title: <u>My Pet</u> _____

_____

_____

_____

_____

_____

_____

_____

_____

_____

ANIMALS, ANIMALS

TALK TO THE ANIMALS

Name _____   Date _____

Pretend that your pet or favorite animal can talk. Write a story about a day with your talking animal.

title: _____, the Talking _____

_____

_____

_____

_____

_____

_____

_____

_____

_____

_____

SHELLO

FRIENDS FOREVER

WHAT IS A FRIEND?

Name _____   Date _____

Friends are very special people. Not only do you have friends, but you are also a friend to others.

1. Is it important to have a friend? Why or why not?

2. What are the most important things a friend can do for you?

3. What are the most important things you can do for a friend?

4. When do you need friends the most?

WANTED: FRIEND

Name _____   Date _____

Pretend you are placing an ad on the school bulletin board trying to meet a new friend. Explain why you would make a good friend and why you would like to have a new friend. Use words such as *kind, funny,* or *loyal* to describe yourself.

WANTED: FRIEND

FRIENDS FOREVER

FRIENDLY PROBLEMS

Name _____   Date _____

1. What would you do if somebody was saying bad things about your best friend?

2. How would you feel if your friend was elected hall monitor and you wanted the job?

3. How would you feel if your best friend was moving away?

FRIENDS FOREVER

FUN FOR TWO

Name _____   Date _____

Make a list of things that are more fun to do with a friend than by yourself.
Use complete sentences.

BEST FRIENDS

Name _____   Date _____

Write a story about how you met one of your best friends.

Draw a picture of you and one of your best friends.

FRIENDS FOREVER

THE PERFECT FRIEND

Name _____   Date _____

Write a story about a make-believe perfect friend. Give him or her a name and tell about his or her likes and dislikes and anything else you'd like to say. Be sure to tell what makes him or her the perfect friend.

LOST AND FOUND

SOMETHING IS MISSING

Name _____   Date _____

Everyone loses things. Write a few sentences explaining how you would handle these problems.

1. You lost the money your friend gave you to hold.

2. You lost your favorite toy.

3. You lost your homework.

LOST AND FOUND

SURPRISE FINDS

Name _____   Date _____

Sometimes we find things that surprise us. Write a few sentences
explaining what you would do if you found these things.

1. You found your favorite pencil sticking out of another child's backpack.

2. You found a bug in a piece of cake during a school birthday party.

3. You found something valuable (jewelry, money)
   next to the sink in the bathroom at school.

LOST AND FOUND

YOU LOST IT, YOU FOUND IT

Name _____   Date _____

Write a paragraph about each of the following.

1. Write about one thing you have lost, how you felt, and what you did.

2. Write about one thing you have found, how you felt, and what you did.

LOST AND FOUND

MAKE A POSTER

Name _____   Date _____

Make a poster to display in your neighborhood that will help find your lost pet. If you don't have a pet, make believe you have one. Be sure to tell readers what your pet looks like, what his name is, and anything unusual about your pet. Also tell your name and how to contact you. Draw a picture of your pet in the box provided.

LOST!

My _____ Name _____

_____

_____
_____
_____
_____
_____

My name _____

My phone number _____

Copyright © Linda Beth Polon

LOST AND FOUND

I'M LOST!

Name _____ Date _____

Have you ever been lost? Write a story about being lost somewhere. It can be in a forest, a mall, an amusement park, or wherever you wish.

LOST AND FOUND

TREASURE CHEST

Name _____   Date _____

Pretend you are a detective. You and a friend are trying to find a lost treasure chest hidden in your town. Write a story to tell about your adventure.

SCHOOL RULES!

I LIKE SCHOOL

Name _____   Date _____

1. Tell what you like about school.

2. Draw a picture that shows when you are the happiest at school. Then tell when and why.

3. Draw a picture that shows when you feel the saddest at school. Then tell when and why.

SCHOOL RULES!

YOUR CLASSROOM

Name _____   Date _____

1. Describe your classroom.

2. What is your favorite place in your classroom? Tell why.

3. What is your favorite thing to do in your classroom?

CREATE STICKERS

Name _____   Date _____

Create stickers or stamps for the people below. Tell why you drew them especially for these people.

1. your teacher

2. your principal

3. your best friend

SCHOOL DAYS

Name _____ Date _____

Write a story about a really great day at school. What would happen? Would you win an award? get all the answers right? make lots of new friends? Tell about your great day from morning to when you leave.

SCHOOL RULES!

I WANT TO BE . . .

Name _____   Date _____

What do you want to be when you grow up? Maybe you should start
working hard now so you can be whatever you want to be.

1. What is your favorite subject in school (reading, math, music,
   something else)? Tell why.

2. What subject are you the best at? How do you know?

3. What do you think you want to be when you grow up?

4. What will you need to study to be able to do this?

I WANT TO BE...

Name _____   Date _____

5. Draw a picture of yourself in your future role.

SCHOOL RULES!

SOLVE THESE PROBLEMS

Name _____   Date _____

1. What should you do at school if you see someone cut into line?

2. What should you do at school if another child hits you?

3. What should you do at school if you see someone take a carton of milk from the cafeteria without paying for it?

4. What should you do at school if someone calls you a name during recess?

5. What should you do at school if someone takes your book?

6. What should you do at school if someone who sits next to you cheats on a test?

MY HOME

Name _____   Date _____

1. Describe your house or apartment.

2. What do you like most about where you live?

3. What do you like least about where you live?

4. Draw a picture of your bedroom.

NO PLACE LIKE HOME

HAPPY AND SAD

Name _____   Date _____

1. Write about and then draw a picture showing something that happens at home that makes you happy.

2. Write about and then draw a picture showing something that happens at home that makes you sad.

TALK ABOUT IT

Name _____   Date _____

Things don't always go the way we want them to.

1. Do you think it is a good idea for families to meet together and talk about problems? Why?

2. If you had a problem at home, whom would you talk to and why?

NO PLACE LIKE HOME

BE AN ARCHITECT

Name _____   Date _____

An architect is someone who designs homes on paper. You can be an architect here! Answer the questions below and then draw a floor plan of your future dream house. A sample floor plan appears below.

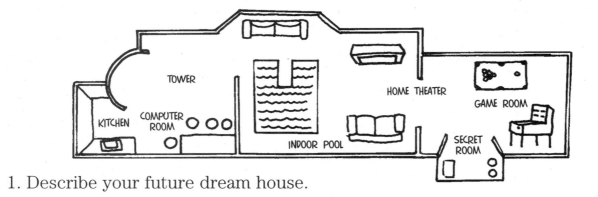

1. Describe your future dream house.

2. What special rooms would you want in your dream house?

Your dream house:

FAMILY TREE: TAKE-HOME ACTIVITY

Name _____   Date _____

Answer the questions below in the space provided and then complete a family tree with your family's help. Some leaves can be blank if you don't have people to list for that category. Add more leaves if you need to.

1. Write down the names of all the children in your family, including yourself. Write the birth dates next to each child's name. If you do not have brothers or sisters, but have a pet or pets, write down their names.

2. List the full names of your mother and father. If you have stepparents as well, write down their names too.

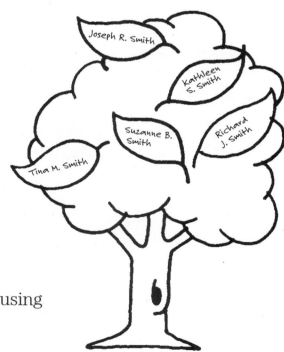

3. Write down the names of your mother's parents and your father's parents.

4. Now add all the names to your tree by using the example at the right.

DRAW YOUR OWN FAMILY TREE

Name _____   Date _____

NO PLACE LIKE HOME

A DAY IN THE LIFE

Name _____   Date _____

Write a story about a usual Saturday in your home. What happens in the morning? Do you eat breakfast with your family? What do you eat? What do you do during the day? What do you do after dinner? When do you go to sleep?

DINOSAURS AMONG US

Name _____   Date _____

Dinosaurs were around a long time ago, before there were people.
Think about what it would have been like to live in the dinosaur age.

1. Would you like to have lived in the dinosaur age? Why or why not?

2. How would your day-to-day life be different now if there were still
   dinosaurs around?

3. When did dinosaurs disappear from Earth?

4. Why do you think they disappeared?

5. Draw a picture of a dinosaur.

BE PART OF HISTORY

THE DINOSAUR NEXT DOOR

Name _____   Date _____

Pretend there is a very small dinosaur living next door to you.

1. Describe how the dinosaur looks. Then draw a picture of you and
   the dinosaur.

2. How would you make friends with the dinosaur? Write a short story
   about your first meeting with the dinosaur next door.

FRONTIER LIFE

Name _____ Date _____

Pretend you live in frontier times. In frontier times you might have lived in a log home on the prairie and attended a one-room school with children of all ages. You might have had many chores to do each day to help out your family. Write about a make-believe day on the prairie in the diary below.

September 10, 1850

Dear Diary,

_____

_____

_____

_____

_____

_____

Sincerely,

_____

BE PART OF HISTORY

I'M AN INVENTOR

Name _____   Date _____

Imagine you are a great inventor. Think about something in your daily life that you don't like, that makes you tired, or that slows you down. Then invent something to fix it. Explain your invention below and then draw a picture of it.

ME FOR PRESIDENT

Name _____   Date _____

You want to be President of the United States.

1. What should you learn in school to prepare to be President?

2. What kind of qualities should a good President have (for example, honesty, kindness)? List at least six. Write in complete sentences.

3. Tell why you would make a good President.

BE PART OF HISTORY

THE GREAT SHIP

Name _____   Date _____

In the early 1900s, many people started moving to this country. They were called "immigrants." Imagine you lived in another country and you have just moved to the United States. Write a story about your ship ride across the ocean to get here. Your journey takes many days and the ship is packed with people. Are you excited? scared? crowded? hungry? Describe how you feel and what you are thinking about.

HOLIDAYS AND CELEBRATIONS

FAVORITE HOLIDAY

Name _____   Date _____

There are many holidays during the year. What are two of your favorite holidays? List them and explain why you enjoy them as much as you do.

1.

2.

HOLIDAYS AND CELEBRATIONS

WE ALL CELEBRATE THE FOURTH OF JULY

Name _____   Date _____

The Fourth of July is one of the holidays that everyone in the United States celebrates.

1. Why do we celebrate the Fourth of July? Do you know another name for the Fourth of July?

2. Why do you like the Fourth of July?

3. What do you do on the Fourth of July? Do you go to a parade? Do you see fireworks? If so, describe the fireworks.

MR. TURKEY'S THANKSGIVING

Name _____   Date _____

Thanksgiving is one of the holidays that everyone in the United States celebrates. Write a story about how a turkey would like us to spend Thanksgiving day. Tell what Mr. Turkey thinks we should do on that day. What do you think Mr. Turkey would like us to eat for Thanksgiving?

GIVING GIFTS

Name _____   Date _____

Some of our holidays and celebrations, such as Christmas, Hanukkah, and birthdays, involve giving gifts.

1. Name two presents you would like to receive and tell why.

    1.

    2.

2. Name two presents you would like to give to other people if you had enough money. Be sure to tell who you would give them to and why.

    1.

    2.

3. Write down the name of each person in your family and the name of your best friend. Then write down something you could do for that person that would not cost anything but that they would appreciate (for example, "clean the kitchen floor for Mom").

HAPPY BIRTHDAY!

Name _____   Date _____

Every year we have a birthday. What age do you think is the best age to be? Write the age in the blank below and then tell why this age is the best. What do you get to do at this age that you can't do now? Then draw a picture of yourself at this age.

My favorite age is _____.

HOLIDAYS AND CELEBRATIONS

CREATE YOUR OWN HOLIDAY

Name _____   Date _____

Is there a holiday you would like to invent? Think about your hobbies and interests and then create your own holiday. For example, you might invent "Cats and Dogs Day," "Eat Only Dessert Day," or "Model Railroad Day." Make up a name for your holiday and then describe below what would happen on your holiday.

My holiday is called _____.

FAVORITE PLACES TO BE

Name _____   Date _____

Our favorite places usually make us feel happy and safe.

1. Where is your favorite place to be at school? Tell why, and draw a picture of yourself there.

2. Where is your favorite place to be at home? Tell why, and draw a picture of yourself there.

MEET ME AT THE FAIR

Name _____   Date _____

Have you ever been to an amusement park or fair? If so, write about a visit to one. What did you ride? What did you eat? What did you see? What games did you play? What was the best part? the worst?

If you have not been to an amusement park or fair, pretend you are going. What will you ride? What will you eat? What games will you play? What do you think the best part will be?

IT'S YOUR AMUSEMENT PARK

Name _____   Date _____

You own your own amusement park, and you want it to be different from other ones. Make up one new ride for your park. Give it a name and tell about it. Draw a picture of the ride.

TRAVEL THE WORLD

WATER, WATER EVERYWHERE

Name _____   Date _____

1. Do you like to go to the beach, the lake, or a swimming pool? Pick which one you like to go to the most and tell why.

2. Do you like to play in the water? What kinds of games do you like to play in the water? Tell about them.

3. Draw a picture of yourself in the water and describe what you are doing.

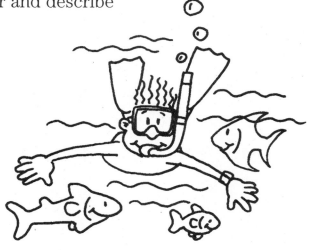

MY BEST TRIP

Name _____   Date _____

What is the best trip you ever went on? Where did you go? Who went
with you? Why was it so great? Tell all about it. Draw a picture of yourself
on your trip.

TRAVEL THE WORLD

MY FAVORITE PLACE TO GO

Name _____   Date _____

If you could go anywhere in the world, where would you go? Why do you want to go there? How would you get there? What would you do there?

TRADE PLACES

Name _____   Date _____

Imagine you could become any person you wanted to be for one day. Who would you choose to be? Tell why you chose this person.

I want to be _____ for one day because

FANTASY FUN

MAKE A WISH

Name _____   Date _____

Pretend you were given three wishes. What would you wish for? Why?

I would wish for _____ because

I would wish for _____ because

I would wish for _____ because

FANTASY FUN

CAN YOU FLY?

Name _____   Date _____

Pretend you have special powers. What are they? Can you fly? Can you clean your room by clapping your hands? What special powers would you like to have and why? Draw a picture of yourself using one of these special powers.

FANTASY FUN

RESTAURANT FOR KIDS

Name _____   Date _____

Pretend you own your own restaurant just for children. Give it a name and tell about the foods you will serve. On another piece of paper, draw a picture of the outside of your restaurant.

My restaurant is called _____.

MAIN MEALS

    1.

    2.

    3.

DRINKS

    1.

    2.

    3.

DESSERTS

    1.

    2.

    3.

WHEN I GROW UP

Name _____   Date _____

What will your life be like when you are a grown-up? Imagine you are as old as your parents. What job do you have? Are you married? Do you have children? How many and what are their names? Do you have pets? Where do you live? What do you do for fun? Write about your grown-up life by answering the questions above.

FANTASY FUN

ANIMAL LIFE

Name _____   Date _____

Pretend you are an animal. You can be a pet, an animal in the zoo, or a wild animal. Tell what you are, where you live, and how you spend your days. Tell what you do, what you eat, and how you feel.

I am a _____.

I live _____.

SEASONS

FALL FROLIC

Name _____   Date _____

Create your own Pumpkin Festival! Answer the questions below and then draw some faces on the pumpkins to enter in a pretend Pumpkin Carving Contest.

1. What kinds of food and drinks will you serve?

2. What kind of games will you play?

WINTER DARKNESS

Name _____   Date _____

In countries near the North Pole, some places are dark during the daytime and nighttime. Write a story about how your day would be different if it were dark all day. Discuss how recess would be different and how after-school activities and sports would change.

SEASONS

SPRING RAINS

Name _____   Date _____

"April showers bring May flowers." It usually rains a lot in the springtime, which helps the grass and flowers grow. What do you like to do when it rains? Write about what you like to do and how a rainy day makes you feel.

SEASONS

A SUMMER TO REMEMBER

Name _____ Date _____

What makes a great summer great? Would you go to camp? Would you
swim every day? Would you sip lemonade and look at your favorite books in
the shade? Write about what you think the perfect summer would be like.

SEASONS

WEATHER SAFETY

Name _____   Date _____

As the seasons change, so does the weather in most places. Some places have scary weather, such as tornadoes. Tornadoes can sweep a whole house away. What kind of scary weather does your state have? List one kind below and then tell what you can do to stay safe when you have that type of weather outside.

We sometimes have _____ in my state.

To stay safe during them we should _____

_____

SEASONS

FAVORITE SEASON

Name _____ Date _____

What is your favorite season: summer, fall, winter, or spring? Why? What do you like to do during that season? Write about your favorite season and then draw a picture of yourself in that season.

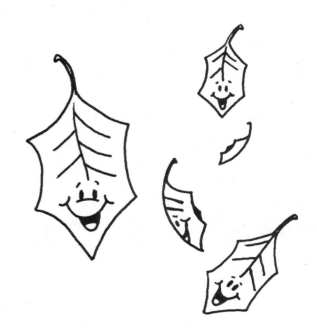

THE HUMAN BODY

THEY ALL WORK TOGETHER

Name _____   Date _____

The body is made up of many parts. Tell how the parts listed below help you every day.

Hands

Eyes

Mouth

Ears

Legs

Nose

THE HUMAN BODY

THE FIVE SENSES

Name _____   Date _____

We learn about the world around us by using our senses: seeing, hearing, tasting, smelling, and touching. For each of the senses listed below, tell about one thing you do every day that this sense helps you with (for example, taste helps you enjoy your breakfast in the morning).

Seeing

Hearing

Tasting

Smelling

Touching

SWEET SOUNDS AND SMELLS

Name _____   Date _____

1. What is your favorite sound? Write about your favorite sound and tell why it is your favorite.

2. What is your favorite smell? Write about your favorite smell and tell why it is your favorite.

THE HUMAN BODY

TAKE A SENSORY WALK

Name _____   Date _____

Ask your teacher or parent to take you on a walk outdoors. Be perfectly silent during your walk. Bring this sheet with you and stop every few minutes to answer the following questions.

1. What do you see? What is big? What is small? What colors do you see?

2. What do you hear? Can you hear birds? airplanes? cars? wind?

3. What do you smell? Can you smell grass? flowers? pollution? food?

4. What can you touch? What does grass feel like? a tree? the sidewalk?

SENSORY SAFETY

Name _____ Date _____

Some smells and tastes can hurt our bodies.

1. Name some things you should NEVER taste.

2. If you, or someone you are with, accidentally tasted something poisonous, what would you do?

3. What is the emergency phone number in your town? How will you help yourself remember it?

SENSELESS

Name _____ Date _____

If you had to give up one of your senses (seeing, hearing, tasting, smelling, touching), which one would you give up? Why? How would you manage without that sense?